HOLD THIS

HOLD THIS
John Martin

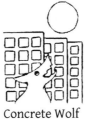

Concrete Wolf
Louis Award Series

Poetry
ISBN 978-0-9964754-4-0

Front cover art: watercolor by Simone Morris-Martin
after a photo by Larry Blackwood

Author photo: by Deborah Ford

Design by Tonya Namura
using Gentium Basic

Concrete Wolf Press
PO Box 445
Tillamook, OR 97141

ConcreteWolfPress@gmail.com

http://ConcreteWolf.com

*Because I have a daughter
and now a grandson who
will live there,
this book is dedicated
to the future.*

*May it always be
better than we deserve.*

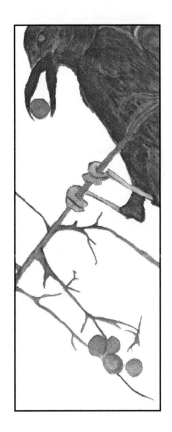

. . . My heart in hiding
Stirred for a bird—the achieve of, the mastery of the thing!
                                              —G. M. Hopkins
                                              The Windhover

Then, in my perverse way, I began to think it wasn't so much
the birds' flying that was exceptional, but this arduous
walking, this dodging and skittering, this strutting and hop-
flying, peck-walking they did among humans. Why humble
themselves so if they could soar like angels?
                                              —Tess Gallagher
                                              Sing It Rough

For to live is to fly, both low and high,
So shake the dust off of your wings
And the tears out of your eyes.
                                              —Townes Van Zandt
                                              To Live Is To Fly

ACKNOWLEDGMENTS

"Lust," "Mission Statement," "Fabrications," "Go," and "Maui," appeared previously, some in different form, in *The Guys' Home Relationship Maintenance and Improvement Poetry Manual*, Two Ravens Publications, 2011.

"Some Days Just Don't Make Any Sense," "Spring In Golden Gate Park," "My Father Says To Me," and "Even The Gleaners" appeared previously, some in different form, in *The Guys' Big Book Of Poetry*, Two Ravens Publications, 2008.

"Anything I Can Do" appeared previously in *Manzanita Quarterly* 6.3 (Spring 2004): 26.

"The Nick Of Time," and "Geology" appeared previously in the chapbook *The Nick of Time*, Iota Press, 2006.

I want to thank the Skyhooks, especially Judith Montgomery, and the High Desert Poetry Cell for helping me shape these poems. Also, the manuscript of this book first came together during a residency at Playa at Summer Lake. Many thanks to Playa.

CONTENTS

HOLD THIS

Just What Happened

What Goes Up

The boy: wanted to hold a bird in his hands.
His hands: bare, small, busy.
His wish: birds could understand his words.
His voice: soft moth wings, low
        so no one else would hear.
His words: I won't hurt you. You're
        safe with me.

He picks up a robin
from the grass. The wiry black feet
feel like letters
traced on his palm.
    He cups a hand beneath
    its orange breast, slides a fingertip
    over its head and down
      between
    the folded wings. He stares into a shining eye,
    sets the robin back in the grass—

            flies up over roofs and trees.

Steward

That a thrush lay headless in the garden
I was paid to care for
troubled me.

No strewn feathers, no sign of struggle, just
that dark red cavity where what belonged
was missing, order simplified to
disorder.

Two black ants there, moving slowly, exploring
this new terrain, waving their antennae,
considering. Otherwise, a perfect bird.

Of course, the stiff legs and feet
looked awkward—useless—as they must
on a dead animal. Woven nest

of vanity, this body, the small heat, those shining eyes
gone into another mouth—and nothing to do now
but bury the remaining

beauty.

The Bundle

The June sun, warm on my shoulders, felt like sprouting wings.
I was expanding, about to lift into the air.
Walking home from the last day of school.
I was eight, we lived in Michigan that year.
Summer was an endless field and I stood at its edge.

A man up ahead was digging a hole next to the sidewalk.
Then he jumped into the hole and struggled with something.
I liked digging holes, finding tree roots, red beneath their skin.
He stood up holding a bundle, like a baby, but wrapped.
It was tied with the string I'd seen at butcher shops.

The man looked at me and smiled.
He reached his arms out, said, "Here, hold this."
Said it like he was asking a huge favor of me.
I set down my armful of papers, all my year's schoolwork.
I put my arms out and he gently placed the bundle on them.

Climbing out of the hole, he said, "I'll be right back."
He walked between two houses and disappeared.
I waited a long time, worrying that I might drop the bundle.
It was very light, light enough to blow away.
My arms began to ache, so long in one position.

Suddenly the bundle moved, as if a bird inside were trying to
    flap its wings.
Then it stopped. Maybe it hadn't even happened. How could it?
I stared at the bundle, waiting for it to move again.
It felt heavy now, I imagined a dead animal inside.
I wanted to put it down but I couldn't disappoint the man.

7

Cars went by but no one stopped. I was whimpering.
I knelt down next to the hole to set the bundle on the grass.
It pulsed again and I yelped, dropped it the last few inches.
I pushed the bundle into the hole with my foot.
I looked around—no one—and began to walk away.

Then I remembered my papers. I wanted to just leave them.
But would the man find them and then find me?
I ran back, tried to grab them, but they scattered.
I managed to wad them all in my arms and I ran toward home.
Was he coming after me? I couldn't look back.

For weeks I stayed away from that block.
One day I was going by in the car with my mother.
The hole was filled, grass was starting to grow over it.
Summer passed, I broke my arm, school started up.
A few months later we moved again, this time down to Florida.

The Nick Of Time

We lived a block from the East River.
Next to that was the Big Tree. My brother
tried to float away from home on a raft.
I was afraid of the dark and the street by the river
where the bully lived. In our backyard were iris,
phlox and bleeding heart. My mother grew peonies,
my father impatient. So we moved to the edge
of town. Across a field the woods began, marching
in place, silently. And next to us the line of oaks
and a lone pine. More bleeding heart, and rhubarb.
Always then it was mow the snow, shovel the lawn,
watch the TV. In April and May water ran along
the gutters under thin ice. People were getting
drunk. People were killing each other. My father
took us to see wrecked cars, the empty shoes still
on the floorboards. My brother built a room
in the basement and locked the door. Our dinner table
had metal legs and we leaned back in our chairs until
we fell over after the third or fourth glass of milk. My
sisters slept late on Saturdays and my father called them
lazy whelps. People were cutting other people's throats,
and the dairy farmers were up early, milking. Ice cubes
clacked and banged in the metal lemonade cooler
at Two Rivers where our picknicking had its heyday.
My brother never came anymore, and the lake began
throwing up dead fish that stank on the beach. We went
anyway; it was our lake. My mother was a nurse and
worked the night shift for the nuns. I put on weight.
The priesthood was a possibility in light of everything.
Birthdays were a big deal, and my parents went into
debt each Christmas, or so my mother told me much
later. Or, maybe not so much later. A few blocks away
I smoked some cigarettes, of course. Then my sister

9

tried to be a nun. Oh, boy. That didn't last long, but
I'll Be Home For Christmas made my mother cry.
The fire chief lived across the street, and my friends
and I would steal matches to start fires in the field of
dry grass next to my house, then madly stamp them out
in the nick of time. That's just what happened.

All Night The Wind Blew

like a hungry ocean at my back,
blew so hard the roof timbers creaked.
It whistled me awake from a dream where
I'd been trying to fall asleep but couldn't because
of all the dogs barking, the racket that those birds made,
so I put a pillow over my head, thought I heard my father
saying something but I couldn't hear his words. All night
the wind blew, and the next morning a silent tongue
of snow had stuck itself through the crack
below the weary door.

Maui

a storm brews to the southwest
above the endless swells and
lightning flickers on the flat horizon
as I leave the beach
having taken my morning swim alone
everyone else here is not alone
everyone else here is in love
of one sort or another
that's what this place is for
that and the bird with one foot
hopping toward me like a drunk
as if life were its ragged joy
as if life were all it had
life with one foot

I tell myself
that I will write about the bird
with one foot knowing as you do
that I will be writing about myself
as the bird hops on past me then
flies to the edge of the surf
lands on the one leg
and sways
dangling what's left of the other
looks out over the waves
with pity in its eye
pity for the ocean
so alone

Anything I Can Do

From the car we walk a path to the river,
sit together on a slab of granite

that turns the water aside.
Mr. Word Power, you call me.

Your head aches again, you say, and your
body, and you feel like you haven't slept

for a week and you've just drunk thirty
cups of coffee. You can't talk, don't

want to talk, don't want me to talk.
Neither of us knows what's

wrong with you, and I've fallen
into the habit of asking,

"Is there anything I can do?"
"See that?" you squint, point at a standing

wave in the middle of the river—
"I want to be painless as water."

On Sunday Morning

Some god,
a very small one, I think, possibly the god of meaningless
patterns or one of those gods-without-portfolio, maybe
one who was just as confused as I, noticed me as I walked
along the frozen lake thinking about how i'm losing you by
wanting you too much, my hunger curdling into anger. I felt
the god pick me up, turn me over, and then, not finding
anything interesting, set me back where I'd been. Well, not
    exactly
where I'd been, because, as we know, the gods can be so
sloppy sometimes, not remembering how things are supposed
    to go.
It's why we try to forget about them, pretend they don't exist—
as if all this could be explained away as heat and light. Energy!
It almost seems we want to punish them for inattentiveness,
give them something to think about the next time
they let themselves get distracted by their imaginations,
by the fantastic worlds they're capable of dreaming up,
sometimes in such detail that they lose sight of what's real
and they plunge headlong into fantasies about beings
like ourselves but smarter, more beautiful, with none
of the infirmities they've given us—oh, I'm sure it's pleasant
to spend time dreaming of such perfect creatures, forgetting
the ones they've actually got, the only ones who care enough
about them to clean up after them, make sure they get to bed
when they've had too much, and then call in sick for them,
tell a little lie that of course no one believes but everyone
pretends to. They're such children, aren't they? Foolish
children who refuse to accept the ways of the world,
the cost of keeping up appearances, the strain, the lengths
we go to for their sake. Well, I suppose their foolishness—

their willfulness too—is understandable if only they'd manage an apology now and then. How hard is that? But, oh, no! Apologize to a human, a pebble in the mud? No, they pick us up, play with us, then drop us without a second thought. It's shameful, really, but what can a person do?

Mission Statement

By dint of luck, by dogged tries,
by belief in no belief, faith in no single
thing, to stumble on and map a reach
of the land of orphan echoes,

by shaping pale sounds that grow wild there
into statues of clouded crystal while
talking with you as two adults would do
about their hopes for the children,

by forsaking my birthright, finding the gumption
to walk upright to the timekeeper as I wipe
my hands on my shirt and inform him that
he's being let go,

by building a hut out of what's at hand in that land
of repetitions and make the decision
to stay, get comfortable with discomfort.
To look in a mirror there and see, of course,

it's two facing mirrors, too many times, to
and fro. To look away, my eyes echoing—
mirrors of the mirror—and then to walk on
toward my vanishing points in search of

true love. Yes, my truest true love,
beyond any vanishing points, where I walk
toward her, and then through her, and
then keep walking toward her.

How To Choose The Right Mirror For You

Stand straight, about your own height out from the mirror,
and stare at the small space between your eyes. Ask yourself,
Are you feeling good right now? Is this the world you want

to live in? What I mean is—if someone offered you money
to kill someone, you'd say, No. Right? But if they said
they'd kill you unless you kill someone, then you should
think

fast about what matters to you, being right or being alive
as you stand before the mirror. Bend your knees, sink down
as far as you can, then rise. Does your image waver like

a charmed snake or a genie escaping from a lamp? And does
seeing yourself this way, as something so strange, leave you
unsteady? Unsure which one is really you, the snake,

the genie or the creature that faced you the last time
you looked in a mirror? If so, buy that mirror now. In fact,
it would even be ok to take it if you don't have

the money to pay for it. Pick it up, put it under your arm,
and if they stop you at the door, tell them it was your
father's mirror, and he wanted you to have it.

Watching For A Sign

Double Exposure

Going through old books of mine, I find a photo.
It's the two of us, taken the last time I saw you alive.

You must be seventy-three there, a year before the end.
Which would make me a man-child of thirty.

I'm hardly tall, but you look like you're crouched beside me
in an overcoat buttoned to the neck and a gray fedora.

Your thin lips resemble an eye held shut, while mine—
thicker and looser—suggest a pleasant sleep.

I seem to hover just off the ground, a blow-up doll,
a dream your body dreamed without asking you.

An open garage door frames us, the space behind us half
shadowed, like your face beneath the brim of your hat.

With your hands hidden in your overcoat pockets, and mine
dangling from the cuffs of a thrift store jacket,

we squint together toward a low-angled sun, neither of us
trusting the lens to see what we want it to.

It's the sort of thing that's left on a shelf when people move,
to be glanced at and then discarded by a stranger.

If someone took that photo of us now, you would not be there
but I would still lean slightly toward you.

After Light Rain

Standing at the kitchen window, spooning yogurt
from its plastic cup, I watch a robin snatch a worm
from the wet concrete, eat it end to end, then
tilt its head and stand very still. Feeling full,
I set the spoon down while the robin hops to a puddle,
looks around and lowers its beak to drink. All morning
I've felt afraid that I might be dying.

Hours later, I'm standing at the window with
a glass of wine, watching another robin hop
through grass I've just cut. It hops six times,
stops, hops five times, stops, looks around,
stabs wildly at the ground, looks around,
raises its head high above its fat chest, like
a presidential portrait, then stabs again. Maybe
I'm just afraid of being alone the rest of my life.

After nightfall I'm washing dinner dishes at the sink,
staring out the window at someone who looks
suspiciously like me. I glance down at the white plate
and the water, and when I look up he's still there.
Almost smiling, he slides a wet hand toward me
through the glass. He has the look of a man who's
trying to forget things before they happen.

Rising Song

How can I love watching the heron
but not love watching it feed?

To watch it wait, still as evening light
for the subtle swell of silver gills,
languid, lucent dorsal fin all unaware,
swaying, as if in rising air—

that's when I want to look away,
not witness what I know.

Then, I'd rather find the flock of sparrows
working a thicket in search of seeds. Have you
ever felt an eyelash flutter on your skin?

That feeling is the sound sparrows make
flaming through the bushes all day long, soft song
that rises to the nest of the sparrow hawk.

My Father Says To Me,

where's the football?
I know what he means—on the front lawn
he will throw and I will run. He will say,
Zing! And I will streak across in front of him,
from left to right and right to left.
He will loft the ball, grunting softly as he
brings his arm forward. I'll catch everything
he throws, two handed, one handed, reaching
behind, diving forward. *You must be tired,*
he'll say after fifteen minutes. I won't be tired at all
but I'll know what he means, so we'll stop.

For a few years I would say to my daughter,
do you want to throw? She knew what I meant—
in the backyard I would crouch and she
would pitch a softball to me, her right arm
describing a great windmill motion, firing the ball
at me as hard as she could. But I loved watching her
more than she loved pitching. Before long
she would say, *I'm tired.* And we would stop.

My father died before my daughter was born,
but when I was young he liked playing catch. *Zing!*
he would say, holding the ball out in front of him
as if it were a gift he'd just been given.

Sky Blues

First there's sky. Lots of it.
It's blue, then gray, then black, then pink, orange, then blue
     again.
But lots becomes too much, so you look down. And when you do
people are making faces, they have numbers on their eyes, giving
you spider looks, looks that make you tired.
But you're busy, happy, building something to hold it all, the sky.
You laugh, laughing is good, it can cure cancer, someone said.
Things are rolling, theories abound, you're in the mix, on your
     game, in
the kitchen. Your body—how wonderful—so much has to go
right all the time, and for you, mostly it does. Sight! How you
     make it up
out of wavelengths and packets of light—photons—even the
     words
are miracles. And your retinal blind spots where you can't see a
     thing
so you just make that part up! You're on the move, at the helm.
     Now and then
the earth shifts, foundations crack, but you wouldn't have it any
     other way. Oh,
there *is* the void—ahead, behind, pretty much everywhere but
     right where
you are. So you try to avoid the void and that's funny, so then
     it's ok.
You can get back to your project with the sky. Which has grown!
     Gone
way over budget—some hard decisions to be made—and just
     then,
your father dies,

of cancer

Oh Boy

Hmmmm

So much to do all the time. And you're not sleeping the way you
used to.

And what's this? While you've been attending to other things
the sky has grown again

like yeast dough, sticking to everything—you, your child (that's
right, that happened),

your little income stream, foreign aggressors, the asteroid with
your name on it—just everything. So that by the time

your mother dies

after you'd assumed she'd live forever

you think, Well

that had to happen, didn't it? And the crying too. Just about
anywhere, especially

in the car. But could this be the road to wisdom? Those tears
maybe cleansing

your own little doors of perception, which—

Holy Cow

there it is, you suddenly see it—

what you've been busy building all this time! Who knew? A door
for the sky, so you

can go through it when you need to. Because you will
need to.

Finch Down

I bend to pick up a house finch
lying on concrete outside my glass door.
My shadow darkens the body as my fingers
slide around it. As if that matters, means
something. And, turning as I stand,
finch in hand, I see my own face
beside the smudge on the glass
and below that a vase of white lilies
that look like they're in my gut.

My bird book says the finch's flight call
is a soft, husky *fidlip* or *vweet*. I tend to fall
in love with a soft, husky voice, no matter what
it's saying. I wonder, was it calling as it hit,
or hearing some other finch's soft, husky *fidlip*?

Dead Dog

As a child I taught our little black mutt
to lie down, roll over and play dead. "Dead
dog," I would say, and she would hold
still on her back, paws up, head to one side,
watching me for a sign.

Then I grew up, moved away,
and one day my mother called
to tell me the news
that had been biding its time.

This morning I agreed that our old tan mutt,
nearly blind, mostly deaf, arthritic,
without control of certain functions,
should be euthanized. Something to do
with quality of life.

This afternoon I held him in my lap
while his quality of life got improved,
then I rolled the body gently onto a table,
watching it for a sign.

Last Camp

After a shooting star at the shore, and her asking me,
"That star—did that actually happen long ago?"
And me explaining what I know, that the Maya
thought shooting stars were gods throwing down
cigar butts—after that conversation we follow

flashlight beams along a ghost path back
to our tent and the embers of our evening.
As we brush our teeth, spit into the dark,
prepare for a last night in camp, I recall
her crawling between her mother and me.

Now, in my sleeping bag, beside this girl about
to depart for her life, I know nothing of where-from
or where-to. I want to tell myself there are no
endings but the ones we invent, no
doors to close but the ones we build.

Morning will come, we will stir from what
we know as sleep. We'll paddle out together
in the kayaks one last time, two floating souls
with no particular goal—just a return to the sandy
spot where we put in.

The Path Dies Out Here

Bear In Mind

A bear is chasing me through a meadow
and I'm running as fast as I can but
he's gaining on me—it seems
he's always gaining on me.
I'm running and running but also
thinking I should just
turn around and say,
"Stop it! Stop chasing me. We both
know you aren't going to catch me.
All you can ever do is chase me. So,
think about it—why bother?"

The bear does stop,
and he sits on his haunches and thinks,
or seems to think. And then
the bear says to me,
"I have to chase you, you know
that. Or you should. And, sure,
we both know I'll never catch you.
So, why not give us both a break and
just stop thinking about me?"

But, with that said, he gets back on four feet,
sticks his long pink tongue out, licks down
both sides of his snout. Then he sighs, looks
behind himself, then at me and says, "Okay,
ready when you are."

Hunger

This morning, when the scrub jay noticed
something and took off from the railing,
its beak stuffed as full of bread crumbs
as it could possibly get, one of the white
pieces dropped, and in a gentle arc of its own,
disappeared into the snow. The jay never dipped or
veered or in any way altered its flight. I saw in
that moment of pure movement and pure
disregard, that no bird would ever feel gratitude
to me for putting bread on a railing, for attending
to its life.

All I can tell you is, this moment you
made room for, cleared a space for at your
table, could be the scrub jay's beak
full of what it's found, or it could be
those other moments you imagine of black
loss down the silent throat of death. It could be
this full moment or that other, one that you
will live anyway when it comes, when it finally
drops from the beak of a bird that never veers
from its course, never looks down at you,
drops over and over, while yet another scrub jay lands
and drums on the railing with its black beak, hungry too.

Here's What I'm Thinking:

                                        that if I could just
find the right moment—some time when
lots of other things are happening but not
important ones, things like standing around with you
and some friends waxing skis and drinking beer,
and me about to leave to go do some things—
unimportant things, but necessary, like food shopping
or housecleaning—things that sometimes I'm happy
to do and sometimes just keep me
from screaming—
            I'm thinking, if just then
I could turn to you, give you a hug and say, "You know
I'm still in love with you," and say it with a brilliant smile,
as if I were remembering something delicious I'd forgotten
to put on my shopping list—if I could just do that right—one
take—then maybe I would somehow, by subtle diligence,
find myself in the back room of your heart where the deals
are made—all it would take then would be the right word
at the right moment from me, and we could all raise a glass
to the new regime, the Pax Amor in your heart—
                                        but wait,
I did all that, didn't I? The day with the snow
and the beer, and softly, so the others couldn't hear,
I murmured those words about stillness and love in your
ear, and you were smiling because, really, you do have some
affection for me, and then I drove away, having learned
that I can manage—subtly, of course—to not learn
anything I don't want to. But maybe, one of these days,
I'm thinking, while distracted by the latest headline or bank
balance, I just might manage to slip into the smoky back room of
my own heart where, if I play my cards right—lay them out on
    the table

for all to see, admit that I want you so badly and I don't even
    know why—
maybe then there'll come that perfect moment when I'll lay
    a hand on my
own shoulder, and as I turn to look up from the cards, there
    I'll be,
smiling that little 'come on' smile, and then I'll agree, silently,
    finally,
to come home with me.

Thumbing Through

Having tossed torn out pieces of my home
into a pit of uncritical acceptance
at the town dump, I sit in line, at the wheel
of my truck waiting to pay, staring
at the view of snow-capped mountains
that can be enjoyed from the dump—
a million-dollar view, much better than the one
I've got from my now-improved home. And,
with a twenty dollar bill in hand, I wonder—
have I ever been part of a garbage dump?
Or at least a humble midden left by some small
band of apes—and was I ever a black cricket
one of them ate, or a grasshopper, or a worm,
brown or gray, and so I wonder—who wouldn't—
was I ever green leaves in the mouth
of an herbivore, and then red flesh in the mouth
of a carnivore, and then, *ipso facto*, in how many
piles of scat I've sat, feeling as at home as I do now
in my fine, improved home? But that sort of thought
never stops there, it rises to the grander view
and considers the mountain peaks I've scaled
on the wind or fallen onto from a cloud, and then
flown down from in a glacier or else some mighty
tropical river—wherever tropics were then,
that's where I was—in some fish fin, swaying red
or blue, then dead in the gloomy deep, then
sunk deeper to rise in a grand volcano, shot hot
and fast, and fallen here—right where I sit—though
right here was somewhere else then. Just like
I was somewhere else when I was five and almost
died trying to swim out to that raft in that lake so far
from here, as far as one can get in sixty years,
and I get to thinking that my long life is like

one of those flip-books that I'm no good at flipping
through, always going too fast or too slow to
get it right, get the flow of the pratfall or the bird
flying or the sun going down behind the mountain,
as I lift my foot off the brake, pull onto the scales
that will weigh how much I've left behind
and calculate how much I owe.

Sunrise

You're camping in the mountains with friends and you're
        awake before sunrise,
so you get dressed, go out to watch the sun come up. Leaned
        against a rock
looking east, you remember doing this with your father so
        long ago. That red
sleeping bag he wrapped around the two of you. You leaned
        back into him.
Silence, stillness now. Then, a bird call—three slow notes,
        both lonely and content.
You shiver, wait to hear it again, whistle it back. You have
        the notes but not the feel.

On the ridge of rocks to the east a marmot runs, stops, runs
        again, disappears. Then,
right where you're looking, a dot of white light so sudden
        you're afraid time has gotten
ahead of you. Now it grows and it moves—you're watching
        the sun move! And now
you can't watch it, it's too much sun. Look away, look back,
        look at your boots,
there's a bright yellow spot on them but it's really on your
        eye, where you saw time
moving.

You close your eyes, the spot's still with you, like the feel of
        leaning into your father.
Then, slowly, slowly the spot disappears so you open your
        eyes. Your boots are dusty,
the light is dusty, you start to get up but then you hear it
        again—the bird. Three notes,

39

still dark and sweet, but something missing now. It's paler,
    like all this sunlight,
too much. Others are stirring in their tents, soon you'll talk,
    will you tell them? The bird,
the light? Probably, but it won't be the same. It's never the same.

For You

Little Lady Jesus on Saturday,
the day for shenanigans, the day for
dancing around the holes in the floor.

Little Lady Jesus of the last days,
the very latest last days, why
am I so afraid of my last day?

Little Lady Jesus from beyond our
poor power to add or detract, give us
one more chance. No, two. Three?

Little Lady Jesus of justice for all,
teach us to acquit ourselves well,
teach us to think very slowly.

Little Lady Jesus of revelations, what
will I think of next? Ah! Did you
put that there? Just for me?

Little Lady Jesus of the humble creatures,
ask one of them to talk to me.
In English, please.

Little Lady Jesus, Queen of
Comeuppance and Righteous Wrath—
they went that-a-way.

Little Lady Jesus of simplicity, please
uncomplicate my life. Let me forget
either sex or tomorrow.

Little Lady Jesus with the exasperated look,
I'm sorry but I am what I am.
Don't you love it?

Little Lady Jesus of big favors,
just find one who's happy to be alive
and put her in front of me.

Little Lady Jesus of weights and
measures, I know I don't deserve
one like that, but please?

Little Lady Jesus of unminced words
who lives for stories and dies for lies,
let me always see the truth coming

before it sees me, Little Lady Jesus,
that's all I ask—a brief moment before
what I do has run off with what I am,

and before you take away my life and give
someone else a turn, which I know
you have to do sooner or later, just

please, please give me all the sweet
confusion I can stand, now while I
stand here begging in tongues, Little

Lady, singing a song I don't know and
don't even trust, just because you asked me to,
because you knew I'd be willing to try,

for you, sweet Lady Jesus, amen.

Father To The Man

My father kept the hot water running hard,
heaped the extra shaving cream on the cold water handle
for touch-up work. I'd watch him in the mirror
dragging the safety razor up his neck as if
shoveling light snow, hold the razor
under the hot stream, then clear another path
beside the first. Such pleasant work,
I couldn't wait.

Other mornings he got up late, didn't shave,
sat staring out the window in his undershirt.
Eventually he would go out and re-park his car
so it wasn't half on the driveway and half
on the front lawn. If only I'd known how to drive.
I would have just done that for him.

Spring River Hike

cold dark clouds
osprey waits on a gray limb
cloud moves, osprey blooms

junco by the path
soft but dead, cradled in grass
such naked feathers

bitterbrush, leafless,
fallen pine cones caught in it
where we stood last fall

across the river
two geese on a rock watch me
watch them watching me

wind combs through grass stalks
something must have wintered here
dead leaves, matted, dried

following the river
black beetle marches toward town
inside a footprint

calm eddy near shore
dead insects circle dancing
with brown pine needles

whose home is this place?
whose bed moved in this frost heave?
careful where I step

white churning water
cold wind, clouds, rock ferns shiver
the path dies out here

Reaching Up

The Night It Finally Rained

She put her hand
on my hand
on her mound.
Slow, go slow—slow down,
she murmured like the rain water
running in the roof gutters.
You want all
the night's rain to fall
at once?
But it wasn't like that—
I was afraid the rain
might see it was me
and decide not to fall
at all.

Lust

My hand is empty as I reach up,
emptier as I reach up higher.

Sometimes I think my hand is yours,
your face there between my fingers.

Have you ever picked ripe plums? Yellow
jackets will be picking plums then, too.

So much we could talk about. Pick any star
in the sky. Think of it as a conversation we

could have. But don't think of me as a conversation
or a star. Think of me as a hand. You're licking

my palm. I call to you as I reach up. "Look," I say
"ripe plums, yellow jackets, conversations!"

Oh, but I am wrong. It's your palm and I am licking it,
aren't I? I would have said I'm sorry this spring

or last year, but the plums are ripe now and I am
here, licking the palm you hold out. Your open palm

that held ripe plums, felt their warmth,
their weight, is on the tip of my tongue.

Fabrications

Mornings, I would wake, check if an email had come,
an email from you. I knew it was part of a mistake—
an understandable error, but one that could reveal,
if I chose to see, a man in love with his own desire.
In those cold months I craved any hint of heat—
long warm arms, thighs that could wrap my head

like a silk scarf. I had no need to see what was ahead,
no wish to imagine any wintry scenes to come
or learn the interest rate on such borrowed heat.
I believed then in pleasure—make no mistake,
I still do—but almost saw through my thin weave of desire,
a fabric so flimsy that what it veils it reveals

to an open eye. So, I imagined you to be a revelation,
when I couldn't in fact see even my own head
for the thoughts it was thinking—tawdry desires
that resembled the web of a drunken spider. Come
into your own dream, said the spider to himself—mistaking
ash for flash, fear for sear, hurt for heat.

But you were real, weren't you? Real heart, real heat,
real head, real flesh that so easily revealed
my folly, love's trompe l'oeil, misery's mistake,
just as you revealed your body when we headed
to your house after lunch. And just as I came
to see the world is naked, clothed only in desire.

Is it a question then of what desire I desire?
Now that I have your heart for my heat?
Now that your body is there when I come

back from wherever desire has led me, revealing
itself, weaving shamelessly through my head,
saying, "Go on, make another lovely warm mistake."

Plenty of heat, not enough warmth—that's the mistake
I always make, but I see it too late—when only desire,
in a scanty get up, is still around. And I do get up, head
off behind it, that blithering spirit that hawks the latest heat
with a threadbare tongue, its sweet revelations
always, like warmth, just about to come.

So, I'll leave my head behind, walk away from that mistake.
Will you come? We'll inch our way through each desire,
touch pockets of hidden heat, feel any part that isn't revealed.

Geology

High in the mountains, far
from you, the air thins

and my thoughts narrow
to just what I'm doing here—

climbing over a boulder big
as a car parked in the scree.

Reaching out my arm,
I grab a ledge of granite

to pull myself up, but
it breaks free in my hand.

I stare at this piece of the world
I've torn off. In my palm

it falls apart again—two fragments
whose rough, glinting surfaces

fit perfectly. I push them
together, pull them apart

before I let them drop.
And it's just now writing this

that I think of us. Then
I thought only what

to do next, where
to put my hands.

Some Days Don't Make Any Sense

Damn dreams. What good are they
when they get it so wrong? Here's
what really happened: she didn't
spread white wings and throw a red sheet
over our heads. She said, "We need to talk
some more." She didn't slide a window open,
reach out and pull in a thin white cloud
to wrap around us—she walked into
the bathroom, pulled some toilet paper off
the roll, and blew her nose. She didn't wake me
at 2am standing next to my bed
in nothing but a red sheet. She said
to me, "I really thought I'd spend
the rest of my life with him." And she didn't
sew silver buttons all over a red sheet
and hand it over, saying, "This
is for us, for our future."
She suggested that maybe
that smell was coming from the back
of my fridge. She certainly didn't
break down and begin to cry
when I reached for her cheek.
She closed her car door,
then waved goodbye
through the windshield.

Cardiology

I thought, it's time to give my heart a rest,
in light of all he's been through these last
fifty plus and then some years. Pack him off
for two weeks on a beach, let the surf
serenade him. Meanwhile, I'd get by
with some sort of bicycle pump or other.
The least I could do for Old Squeezer.

But then I thought, What if the waves
surging in and surging out,
surging in and surging out, remind him
too much of work? What then?
And me, back here,
trying to cope with you,
my thoughts of you, our imagined conversations,
trying to rig up some kind of
sump pump on my belt.

Instead, maybe I should buy him a ticket to Paris,
City of Light and Love and the Louvre.
And Notre Dame and Sacre Coeur.
City that we've never been to
because we've never been anywhere.
That could be good for my heart, but
what if it were so good he refused
to come back? What if he arranged,
unbeknownst to me, as they say,
a rendezvous in some arrondissement
no one's ever been to?
        Certainly not us.
I think that then my heart would break, willy-
nilly. At least, I'd want him to.

No, I'd best leave well enough alone—
just give him an hour like this to go off on his own,
an hour when I have nothing important to do,
because, with you still somewhere around
I need my heart more than ever before—
left, right, left, right—keep me more
or less on message—you demon from Hell!

See? I can't be trusted to go two feet
without Mr. Reliable keeping the beat,
that restful rhythm, that lullaby
of now and now and now and now.

Resolution

So, goodbye,
to us, to my year of trying,
to what happened instead
of what wouldn't.

To that February dinner
we got high and drove
through the black night
and ate like happy fools—
how you glowed in that low
cafe light and how we talked
so much and so well, goodbye.

Or that sunny May Monday
after work, sitting on my
rented porch in ugly chairs
I'd found somewhere
sharing red wine, me
already knowing I had
no chance but thinking instead
how little we really know
about what we know. Oh,
my.

To Sunday in July, lounge chairs
on your patio, the newspaper
here and there, you asleep, your
cheek smudged from gardening,
your sagging upper arms
bare and me wanting so
to kiss that spare flesh
but aware I'd rouse you
from your sunny drowse,

and you didn't want
such things from me.

Still, that October hike
up on Broken Top, cold
and bright as clouds
moved in, last chance
before the snow. And later,
over Spanish coffee
I heard it coming—
you paused, said, "So,
I've decided . . ."

            Now,
a whole year of days to come,
ones that I worked hard
so you would want
to live them with me—
instead, this almost weightless
goodbye. The same days I saw,
but so differently.

Last Year's Garden

That bright pink string we wound around our tripod
of sticks, then wove beans and peas through as they grew
has faded to gray, stretched and sagged, some dried tan vines
still holding tight. I took a photo of it yesterday.

A few late tomatoes, caught by frost, are white ghosts
of winter-flattened skin, half hid amid tangled stalks.
And you—so new to it all then—I got to show you
how I plant, how I weed, how I wait.

The rosemary died. I have no luck with rosemary here.
I might get a few raspberries this year. Remember
when you asked me about the *hollycocks?*
We laughed at that, didn't we? We laughed a lot.

Out next to the rows of carrots that I pulled after
you left, a few onions and leeks survived the cold—
still small even now but I'll dig them soon, cook
a spring meal for my daughter who's moved back home.

Her dog keeps badgering me as I try to write. Wants me
to throw him his rubber bone. Last throw hit the trunk
of the sour cherry tree. It's well budded, I see,
could supply some pies if I do the tedious work

I didn't do last June. He's a digger though, a disturber
of the peas. (You always liked my puns. It must
have been something else.) So, I guess
I'll need a fence if I plant a garden this year.

After The End Of That

Find a new love, but something
you can't feel humming inside

your bones. No—not a dog,
not anything with an ending.

Maybe a foreign language.
Say your name, all of it,

out loud, at least once a day.
Don't abuse mirrors and

don't wear your brain out
explaining. Look up, if you

need to, the age, size and
direction of the universe.

Breathe, stare when necessary, beware
your own advice, keep regular

habits, and, whenever you're hungry
remember: love is the fish,

truth is the river.

Something At The Far End

Spring In Golden Gate Park

Mid walk at the arboretum a hawk
flew from a blur at the corner of my eye—
or, not so much my eye, more my thoughts.
"See that? It's got something!" My friend stopped short.
I turned and looked—for what? So hard to see
a sight you don't expect. Low in a tree
we'd just guessed was a type of flowering plum
a dead mole hung head-down across a limb.

And pinning it in place, the hawk stared out
at all the world, but mostly stared at me,
then bowed its head. One rip, two rips, then three.
So, life went on as we two strolled about.
A hawk, a mole—I thought about the luck
to live and look and eat and think and talk.

Plums

This sparrow looks dead,
breast down, wings spread,
at rest, its delicate spine bared
below the twisted head.

A cat, I suppose, waited
under the plum tree, neither
patient nor impatient, but
cat-like, and carried its fruit
here to this stone step
for cat-like delectation.

More ants than I can count,
small, wine-dark and seething,
have found their future
beneath the sheltering wings.

Their wiry legs step through feathers
and push beneath dangling sparrow-down
to reach the table that's been laid.

And I, on my way
to pick plums, have found
instead this feast.

The tiny eyes and beak are solemnly closed
and a lost breeze stirs a loosened feather.

But now, like the slow, beating birth
of a third wing, more feathers rise
then fall, together, and
as if to itself, the small head
nods slightly up and down.

Up and down, though the blood is dried
along the ivory spine. Pale and soft
and squirming with purpose, new lives
hatch in this sparrow head.

Who has not been told that what is done
is done? Who has not heard
that each thing ripens in its own time,
and when the moment is right
sweet juice might run from your lips?

Take it all, like a plum, in one mouthful.
Close on it slowly.
Do not refuse this feast. Say, thank you.

Go

On a walk along the river I'm finally
seeing how to say good-bye to you
months after you've said it to me, when

a late summer rain begins, bringing
the dark water to a simmer. I shelter
under a pine, watch a kingfisher shout

at its children, chase them from home—
Go! Find your own! Only so much
can be handed over from one life to another.

Find your own stretch of river. But then,
I wonder, do their calls echo, flights
overlap, looks cross?

Love takes so many forms, can only take
forms, cannot exist purely as love itself—
while we can exist only as forms—

the form of a kingfisher, keen to feed
and breed, then chase away its own.
The form of a broom in the shape of a bird—

Away with you! Love says, Go!
Or as the current of a river, where I've put
my ear, heard the rain going down—

down, until light and heat lift it again,
transform it, as fish is lifted into air,
transformed to feather and wing.

O, I would have love lift me up, here
and now, into a kingfisher new
to the game—or, better yet, this rain,

starting again its long love affair,
passing through all the forms, even running
through my brain as that love I speak of,

unable to think for itself, but
inclining me to stand here alone
transforming you, the rain, the river,

the glinting fish, the kingfishers young
and old, and the eye in all of this—
the local forms of love.

Like Always

I park in the garage, close the door
behind me, walk through the kitchen,
down the hall to the room where he's asleep,
cough, take off my coat, set down the keys,
lay the hand he knows so well a half-
inch from his snout and watch as
his even breathing doesn't miss a beat.

His ears are nearly empty. His eyes,
when open, tend to stare. Now, finally,
even the hand of god has lost its scent.
"There are worse things in this world,
which doesn't stop for dogs and never will."
I pretend he says that to me, idly smoothing
fabric with his paw while he speaks.

He's mentioned to me more than once
how he wanders so far off in sleep that,
climbing back awake again, he wonders
if it's still his own or a stranger's house
he's woken in, where each present thing
is as it was, but he's become
some other dog in someone else's skin.

Blue

The vet, for some reason,
sterilized the point of injection,
then slid the needle in,
pushed the lethal red liquid
into his vein. His own limping
heart did the rest of the work,
pumping it home, shutting
down the works.

Last night I slept nine hours,
and this first morning
of his death the sky
is so clear, such a bottomless
light blue, it could mean
almost anything.

Even The Gleaners

Folded lightly into a wheelchair,
knuckles too big now, chest too small,
an avalanche of skin beneath
milk-washed eyes. This ninety-five
is not a ripe old age. It's what's
left of you, what even the gleaners
didn't take.
Those thighs that welcomed me
to this world, that must have been fields
of light even to my closed eyes,
are swathed in a plastic diaper now.
You stare at me, head tilting back,
chin wagging out of control. And then,
a thought buds in spring,
takes weeks to branch across
your face. You smile at your own
joke before you say, "My
baby."
We are in a long narrow hallway,
and I have to look up
for something
at the far end.

1908–1982

Really, my memory isn't that good, I don't trust it,
but I'll say it was the last time I talked to him. It was
on the phone, which hung on the wall then. He told me
from his hospital bed—and let me say I have never been
able to picture him in that bed, never—he told me he had just
had a piece of his birthday cake—it was his last—and his voice
was very weak, the sound of an insect walking across glass,
so weak that I couldn't imagine him opening his mouth
wide enough to get a bite in. But he told me that the cake
had been very good, and in his raspy scratch of a voice he
     managed
somehow to suggest a moist sound of cake that made me happy
for him. Now, I don't remember if he told me that it was
chocolate cake or any of those details that he liked to talk about.
And I don't remember the rest of what we said to each other—
     in fact
I don't remember a single thing I said to him, and I'm not going to
make something up. What I remember is where I was, which was
a long way from him, and that a month and a half later my sister
called me through that same phone on the wall, and that was that.

Heart Murmur

He slept with her, these nights he sleeps alone.
In his twitching dreams coyotes wail and yip.
She loved her dog but now she's gone, she's grown.

They howl sweet hell to him, sirens of a different dawn.
And he's loping toward them, pink tongue, grinning lip.
Except for dreams, these nights he sleeps alone.

The lumps, the rheumy eyes, the sigh and groan—
she isn't there to see the gimpy hip.
They shared their youth but now she's gone, she's grown.

No dreams of what he doesn't own.
No pockets for the past. No hollowed grip.
He turns in circles, sleeps or doesn't sleep, alone.

It's a heart murmur will finally take him down,
though pills can buoy his slowly sinking ship.
In life we chart a course, we go, we're gone.

With every breath he swallows another stone.
And the weight his heart's been holding starts to slip.
He slept with her, these nights he sleeps alone.
She loved her dog but now she's gone, she's grown.

Poem

Father, loss, trees, dusk, home,
blood, birds—I write the same poem
over and over. Happiness has slipped away
under suspicious circumstances.
Death has a cramp from crouching
so long in the same patient position.

My father was bitter and so
I failed him, but not for long
because I'm afraid of failure.

I would choose to be a bird instead,
to get away from all of this. If I
were a bird I wouldn't even need to think
about that choice. Plus,
the views.

It's always dusk—I don't care
what time it is. Where I am
it's dusk, and soon we can all just
give up and go to bed. There's safety
in covers. And when I finally do
make it back home you won't see
much of me. Why risk leaving again?

Oh yeah, sex—put that
up in line two with blood and birds.
Or somewhere in place of happiness.

Now, trees—they're my heroes.
Their tenacity and indifference,

their hospitality to birds. I've cut down
my share of trees.

And blood—a little goes a long way. Like
fire, you want to get close but not
too close. Because each of us
is a lot of blood in one place, a lot
to lose. And everything, everything
keeps coming
to its end.

About the Author

John Martin grew up in Wisconsin where he first started playing around with words. When he was old enough to vote and get drafted into the military he moved to Los Angeles and enrolled at Immaculate Heart College. Four years later he had a degree in English Literature, the Vietnam War had ended and he had one published poem to his credit.

Two years after that he moved to northern California where he became a landscaper to pay the expenses that poetry didn't quite cover. He began writing essays and prose fiction more than poetry but only managed to publish one essay in the San Francisco Chronicle.

A move to Bend, Oregon, renewed his interest in poetry, and in 2006 Iota Press published his chapbook, *The Nick of Time*. He also wrote articles for the Bend Bulletin and Bend Living Magazine. Along with other members of the High Desert Poetry Cell, he contributed to three anthologies: *The Guys' Big Book of Poetry*, *The Guys' Home Relationship Maintenance and Repair Poetry Manual*, and *Braided Rivers*. His poems have also appeared in *Manzanita Quarterly*, the *High Desert Journal*, *The Cascades Reader*, and *America Magazine*. This book is his first full length poetry collection.